# Korean
## phrasebook

lonely planet

**Kevin Chambers**
with the help of
**Sim Chambers**

**Korean Phrasebook**

**Published by**
  Lonely Planet Publications
  Head Office: PO Box 88, South Yarra, Victoria, 3141, Australia
  Also: PO Box 2001A, Berkeley, CA 94702, USA

**Printed by**
  Colorcraft, Hong Kong

**Korean script typesetting by**
  All Languages Typsetting & Printers Pty Ltd, Marrickville, NSW

**First published**
  May 1988

| | |
|---|---|
| Editor | Mark Balla |
| Design, cover design & illustrations | Joanne Ryan |
| Typesetting | Ann Jeffree |

National Library of Australia Cataloguing in Publication Data

Chambers, Kevin
  Korean phrasebook

  ISBN 0 86442 060 9

  1. Korean Language – Conversation and phrase books – English. I. Title.
  (Series: Language survival kit).

495.7'83'421
© Copyright Lonely Planet, 1988

# Contents

**INTRODUCTION**   5

**PRONUNCIATION** Vowels – Consonants – Intonation   6

**GRAMMAR** The Sentence – Negatives – Yes & No   10
– Pronouns – Questions – Verbs – Tense – Nouns
– Place Words

**GREETINGS & CIVILITIES** Attracting Someone's   16
Attention

**SMALL TALK** Family Terms – About Yourself   19
– Feelings – Some Useful Phrases

**ACCOMMODATION** Some Useful Phrases – Some   26
Useful Words – At the Laundry

**GETTING AROUND** Directions -Instructions – Some   32
Useful Phrases – Some Useful Words

**AROUND TOWN** At the Post Ofice – At the Bank   37
– Emergencies

**IN THE COUNTRY** Animals – In the Country   44
– Weather – Place Names

**FOOD** Mealtimes – Drinks -Fruit – Seafood – Meat   48
– Vegetables – Condiments – Other Food – Some
Useful Phrases – Some Useful Words

**SHOPPING** Bargaining – Quantities – Information    5●
– Colours – Some Useful Phrases – Some Useful
Words

**HEALTH** At the Chemist – Parts of the Body – Some    6●
Useful Phrases

**TIME & DATES** Telling Time – Months – Days    6●
– Some Useful Phrases – Some Useful Words

**NUMBERS** Some Useful Words    7●

**VOCABULARY**    7●

# Introduction

Korea is one of the most ethnically homogeneous countries in the world. Virtually every citizen of Korea is an ethnic Korean and speaks Korean. A small number of ethnic Chinese (about 50,000), most of them from Shandong province, could be considered Korea's only minority.

The Korean language is a member of the Ural-Altaic language family which also includes languages as diverse as Mongolian and Turkish. The language has been spoken in one form or another for over 5000 years, but was not written until the phonetically based alphabet, *hangŭl*, was invented by King Sejong in the mid 15th century.

Koreans are very friendly people, especially toward visitors. Although some Korean customs may strike outsiders as rude (like failing to hold doors open for others), Koreans are unsurpassed when it comes to playing host.

Outside of Seoul, it is difficult to find people who speak more than a few English words. Your best bet for locating English-speakers is to look for university-aged Koreans or the staff at tourist hotels. The Koreans are cheered by any effort to learn their language, and a little Korean will get you a long way in this nation of 40 million people (North Korea has another 30 million).

This book is designed to help you travel independently. You will have an immediate advantage over other travellers in Korea, especially when outside the major centres. With reduced language difficulties, the success of your travels in Korea will be in your hands.

Good luck in your travels. *Haeng'un ŭl pimnida!*

5

# Pronunciation

Spoken Korean is quite unlike the languages of neighbouring China and Japan. Written in a unique phonetic alphabet (*hangŭl*) developed by King Sejong in the 15th century, written Korean is very easy to learn . The phonetic letters or components are grouped into syllables which may look like Chinese ideograms to non-Korean speakers. Although Koreans still make use of Chinese characters, especially in newspapers, the much simpler *hangŭl* is increasingly used to the exclusion of Chinese ideograms. Many foreigners feel that once learned, the Korean alphabet is much easier to use than the romanised versions.

Throughout this phrasebook you will find both the *hangŭl* and the popular McCune-Reischauer romanisation system used side by side. I encourage you to use the following chart to memorise the 24 letters of the Korean alphabet. It will make your stay in Korea much more pleasant.

Korean contains several sounds not found in English so the examples given should be considered only as close approximations. The best way to learn exact pronunciations is to listen to native speakers.

## Vowels

| | |
|---|---|
| a | a as in 'car' |
| ya | ya as in 'yard' |
| ŏ | a as in 'about' |
| yŏ | yea as in 'yearn' |
| o | o as in 'home' |
| yo | yo as in 'yoke' |
| u | o as in 'do' |
| yu | you as in 'you' |
| ŭ | e as in 'taken' |
| i | i as in 'ink' |

## Combinations

Vowels sometimes occur together in syllables but are usually pronounced separately. Thus 'oe' will sound something like the English word 'way'. On the other hand, 'ae' is a single sound.

| | |
|---|---|
| ae | a as in 'hat' |
| yae | ya as in 'yam' |
| e | e as in 'ten' |
| ye | ye as in 'yes' |
| oe | wa as in 'way' |
| wi | wi as in 'wield' |
| ŭi | u + i |
| wa | wa as in 'waffle' |
| wŏ | wo as in 'won' |
| wae | wa as in 'wax' |
| we | we as in 'wet' |

## Consonants

Korean consonants can assume different sounds according

to their position in the word. For example, the Korean letter
ㄱ can sound like an English 'k' if it appears at the
beginning of a word but sounds more like 'g' if it appears
between vowels.

Aspirated consonants have an apostrophe after the romanised letter and should be pronounced with extra breath.

| Korean Letters | Initial | Romanisation Medial | Final |
|---|---|---|---|
| ㄱ | k | g | k |
| ㄴ | n | n | n |
| ㄷ | t | d | t |
| ㄹ | r | r | l |
| ㅁ | m | m | m |
| ㅂ | b | b | p |
| ㅅ | s | s | t |
| ㅈ | ch | j | t |
| ㅊ | ch' | ch' | t |
| ㅋ | k' | k' | k |
| ㅌ | t' | t' | t |
| ㅍ | p' | p' | p |
| ㅎ | h | h | ng |

## Double consonants

Double consonants are said with a tenser feeling in the
throat.

| | | | |
|---|---|---|---|
| ㄲ | kk | gg | k |
| ㄸ | tt | dd | – |
| ㅃ | pp | bb | – |
| ㅆ | ss | ss | t |
| ㅉ | jj | jj | – |

**Complex consonants**

These consonants occur only in a medial or final position in a word.

| ᆪ | – | ks | k |
| ᆬ | – | nj | n |
| ᆭ | – | nh | n |
| ᆰ | – | lg | k |
| ᆱ | – | lm | m |
| ᆲ | – | lh | p |
| ᆳ | – | ls | l |
| ᆴ | – | lt' | l |
| ᆵ | – | lp' | p |
| ᆶ | – | lh | l |
| ᆹ | – | ps | p |

## Intonation

There is little variation in stress or pitch in Korean. Syllables should be pronounced with almost equal stress.

# Grammar

## The Sentence

The basic word order of a Korean sentence is subject-object verb. Rather than say:

'Who painted that picture?'

a Korean would say something like:

'Who that picture painted?'

Koreans tend to omit any information from the sentence which they feel should be obvious to the situation. The subject is often omitted from spoken Korean and it is not uncommon for the verb to comprise the entire sentence.

Although the Subject-Object-Verb order is rigid, the addition of details such as place and time is more flexible. In general, the more important the information is, the closer it is placed to the verb. Koreans who speak English sometimes carry over the tendency to omit the subject of a sentence when speaking English leaving some listeners wondering who or what is being spoken about.

## Negatives

To simply say 'no', say *aniyo*. To make a sentence negative use the abbreviated version *an* in front of the verb thus:

| | |
|---|---|
| I go. | *nanun kayo* |
| I do not go. | *nanun ankayo* |

Do not use *an* in front of *isseyo*, the verb meaning 'to exist'. Instead use the verb *ŏpseyo* 'doesn't exist':

| | |
|---|---|
| We have beansprouts. | *k'ongnamul isseyo* |
| We don't have beansprouts. | *k'ongnamul ŏpseyo* |

If you want to say that you 'never' do something then use the word *mot*:

| | |
|---|---|
| I never eat meat. | *nanun kogi mot mŏgŏyo* |
| Mr Lee can't go. | *lee sŏnsaengi mot kayo* |

Koreans sometimes use more elaborate sentence structures for negative sentences but you should be able to communicate effectively even with a limited repertoire.

## Yes & No

To say 'yes' to a question you need only repeat the verb. To say 'no', repeat the verb, placing *an* before the verb or use one of the other negative forms outlined.

## Pronouns

| | |
|---|---|
| I/me | *nanŭn* |
| you | *tangsin* |
| he/him | *kŭnŭn* |
| she/her | *kŭnyŏnŭn* |
| we/us | *uriga* |
| they/them | *kŭdŭl* |
| it | *kŭgŏsŭn* |
| this | *ige* |
| these | *igŏtdŭl* |

| that | *kŭke* |
| that (far away) | *chŏge* |
| those | *kŭgŏtdŏl* |
| who/whom | *nugu* |

It is generally impolite to use the word 'you' *tangsin* when talking to someone. Whenever possible, omit personal pronouns from the sentence.

## Questions

| who | Who are you? |
| *nugu* | *nugu'simnigga?* |
| which | Which one is better? |
| *ŏnŭ* | *ŏnŭ kŏsi tŏ chosŭmnigga?* |
| what (pron) | What are you doing? |
| *muŏt* | *muŏt hasimnigga?* |
| where | Where are you going? |
| *ŏdisŏ* | *ŏdi kasimnigga?* |
| when | When are you going? |
| *ŏnje* | *ŏnje kasimnigga?* |
| how | How do you feel? |
| *ŏddŏk'e* | *kibuni chom ŏttŏsimnigga?* |

Notice that when the suffix *-imnigga* is attached to the end of the verb stem it indicates a question. The suffix *-imnidda* added after the verb stem indicates a statement. Although these rules are useful in determining whether you've heard a question or a statement, not all questions and statements use this form.

## Verbs

Although only three verb tenses exist in Korean – past,

present and future – there are a number of verb forms which are used according to the relative formality between the speakers. The forms used range from very formal to quite impolite forms used only for speaking to dogs and children. For safety's sake this book includes only the formal and polite forms.

Here's an example of these two forms:

*kasŭmnida* to go (formal)
*kayo* to go (polite)

The polite *-yo* style is the most generally used form but you cannot err by using the most polite formal or *-sŭminda* style.

Korean verbs do not indicate person or number. *Kasŭmnida* may mean any of the following:

> I am going.
> You are going.
> He/she /it is going.
> We/they are going.

## Tense

Tense rules can be complicated when combined with verb forms but the following will give you an idea of how tense is handled in the polite *-yo* form:

| Verb stem | Past | Present | Future |
|---|---|---|---|
| eat | ate | am eating | will eat |
| *mŏg–* | *mŏgŏsseyo* | *mŏgŏyo* | *mŏgkessoyo* |

Varying tenses of verbs have been given where necessary. To reduce the chance of being misunderstood, place a time word before the verb (usually between the subject and the object). A list of time words can be found in the chapter called 'Time & Dates' but here are the most common words:

| | |
|---|---|
| yesterday | *ŏje* |
| today | *onŭl* |
| tomorrow | *naeil* |

## Nouns

Korean nouns do not indicate number. *Hakkyo* can mean 'a school', 'the school', or 'schools'. There are no articles used with nouns in Korean. Nouns are followed by particles which show whether the noun is the subject, object, or place of action in the sentence. If the noun is the subject, it is followed by *ga*, *i*, *ŭn*, or *nŭn*. If it is the direct object, *ŭl* or *rŭl* are added after the noun. *Esŏ* is added after the noun if it is the place of action in the sentence. For example:

| | |
|---|---|
| The house is large. | *chip-ga k'ŏyo* |
| I see the house. | *chip-ŭl pwayo* |
| I work at the house. | *chip-esŏ ilhaeyo* |

Don't let the particles intimidate you. Virtually everyone will be able to understand your meaning even if you omit the particles.

## Place Words

These common place words are used after nouns to indicate relative location:

| | |
|---|---|
| above | *wi* |
| behind | *twi* |
| below | *arae* |
| beside | *yŏp'* |
| front | *ap'* |
| inside | *sok* |
| next to | *taŭm* |
| outside | *pakka* |

The particle *e* usually follows these place words.

It's under the desk.
  *ch'aeksang arae-e issoyo*

It's in my pocket.
  *chumŏni sok-e issoyo*

# Greetings & Civilities

One of the first things you will notice about Koreans is the degree of propriety with which they conduct themselves with others (in one-on-one situations). Whether you are in Seoul or the remotest village, the Koreans exhibit a natural politeness and strict adherance to the rules of etiquette. Observe Korean etiquette to make a good impression and to preserve the other person's all-important 'face'.

The all-purpose Korean greeting of *annyŏnghashimnika* can be used at all times of the day and in situations in which we would say 'hello', 'good morning', 'good afternoon', or 'good evening'. This greeting, which literally means 'be in peace' is used formally and in addressing superiors. *Annyŏnghaseyo* can be used in less formal situations. Friends may greet you with *odi kaseyo?* (where are you going?) but they don't expect a report on your destination – a simple 'to the shop' or 'down the street' will do.

Bow slightly when greeting others or when departing. Today, many bows are quick dips of the head. Since personal names are regarded as personal property, use titles rather than names in conversation when possible. Although *sŏnsaeng-nim* literally means 'teacher', it is used as a general title of respect and can be placed after the surname (thus Pak Hyong Sim would be Pak *sŏnsaeng-nim*) as an equivalent to Mr, Mrs, or Miss or it can be used alone and without mention of the person's name. Never use a Korean's given name (the second and third syllables of the name) as it is considered private.

Expressing gratitude with *kamsahamnida* or *komap-*

*sūmnida* is common. In most cases when you would normally say 'thank you', use one of these formal expressions of gratitude.

## *Attracting Someone's Attention*

To get a stranger's attention, Koreans call out with one of several standard kinship terms which vary with the age and sex of the other person. A middle-aged man can be addressed as *ajosshi* (uncle) and a elderly man over 60 can be called *haraboji* (grandfather). For a middle-aged woman *ajumoni* (aunt) is used and a woman over 60 should be addressed as *harmoni* (grandmother). These terms are used when you feel close to the one being addressed or to get the attention of a stranger such as a merchant, a driver, etc.

In a restaurant you can use *yoboseyo* (hello) to get the attention of the waiter or waitress. This word is also useful to announce your presence when entering a room.

Hello.
  *annyŏnghasipnigga*          안녕하십니까?
Goodbye. (staying)
  *annyŏnghi kasipsio*          안녕히 가십시오.
Goodbye. (leaving)
  *annyŏnghi kyeshipsio*        안녕히 계십시오.
How are you?
  *annyŏnghasipnigga?*          안녕하십니까?
How's it going?
  *chaemi ka ŏttŏssŭmnigga?*    재미가 어떻습니까?
I'm fine.
  *ne chossumnida*              네, 좋습니다.
I'm happy to meet you.
  *ch'ŏŭm poepkessŭmnida*       처음 뵙겠읍니다.

Thank you.
*komapsŭmnida*  고맙습니다.

Please.
*put'akhamnida*  부탁합니다.

What's wrong?
*wae kurosumnigga?*  왜 그렇습니까?

No.
*aniyo*  아니오.

Yes.
*ye*  예.

You're welcome.
*ch'ŏnmaneyo*  천만에요.

Excuse me.
*sillyehamnida*  실례합니다.

I'm sorry.
*mianhamnida*  미안합니다.

Good night.
*annyŏnghi chumusipsio*  안녕히 주무십시오.

Hello. (on phone)
*yoboseyo!*  여보세요.

Do you understand?
*asigessŭmnigga?*  알겠읍니까?

I don't understand.
*morŭgessŭmnida*  모르겠읍니다.

I understand.
*algessŭmnida*  알겠읍니다.

# Small Talk

It's easy to strike up a conversation with Koreans – most are not shy and will respond well to you if you take the initiative. Koreans ask a lot of personal questions about family, occupation, background, etc, so learn a few phrases to tell others about yourself. So few foreigners bother to learn Korean that Koreans will be surprised and very pleased to hear you say anything in their language.

In the countryside, foreigners are an uncommon sight and you may find yourself the centre of attention. Elderly citizens may find blond or red hair quite fascinating and children may follow you screeching *mikun* (American soldier) whether you are an American soldier or not.

When you address people, remember not to use their personal names if possible and avoid pointing or gesturing with one finger as this is impolite. Beckoning is done with the palm down and with fluttering fingers.

May I ask your name?
  *sŏnghami ŏttŏk'e*
  *toeshimnika?*              성함이 어떻게 되십니까 ?
How old are you?
  *myŏssal imnika?*          몇 살 입니까 ?

## Family Terms
Terms for relatives often differ according to the sex of the person related. Thus, if you are male, you would call your older brother *ŏnni* while if you are female, you would call him *obba*. To further complicate matters, the terms often differ

19

according to whether you are talking about your own relative or about someone else's. When speaking of someone else's relative, if there is a separate honorific term be sure to use it. When speaking of your own relatives use the honorific terms only when speaking of an older relative.

The first of the two tables following contains a list of terms which have no honorific equivalent, while the second shows those with both possibilities.

younger brother of a man
   *tongsaeng*                동생
younger brother of a woman
   *nam tongsaeng*     남동생
younger sister of a man
   *yŏ tongsaeng*       여동생
younger sister of a woman
   *tongsaeng*                동생
son
   *adŭl*                     아들
daughter
   *ttal*                       말
uncle
   *samchon*             삼촌
aunt
   *sukmo*               숙모
husband
   *namp'yŏn*         남편
wife (one's own)
   *anae*                  아내
wife (another's)
   *puin*                   부인

grandfather
*harabŏji*                      할아버지
grandmother
*harmŏni*                       할머니

| Relative | Ordinary | | Honorific | |
|---|---|---|---|---|
| elder brother | | | | |
| of a man | *ŏnni* | 언니 | *hyŏngim* | 형님 |
| of a woman | *obba* | 오빠 | *orabŏnim* | 오라버님 |
| father | *abŏji* | 아버지 | *abŏnim* | 아버님 |
| mother | *ŏmŏni* | 어머니 | *ŏmŏnim* | 어머님 |
| older sister | | | | |
| of a man | *nuna* | 누나 | *nunim* | 누님 |
| of a woman | *ŏnni* | 언니 | *hyŏngim* | 형님 |

## *About Yourself*

My name is ........
........ *imnida*

… 입니다.

What is your occupation?
*tangsinŭi chigŏbŭn muŏshimnika?*

당신의 직업은 무엇입니까?

I'm a ........
*nanŭn ........ imnida*

나는 … 입니다.

athlete
*undong-ga*

운동가

carpenter
*moksu*

목수

doctor
*ŭisa*

의사

hairdresser
*miyongsa*

미용사

journalist
*kija*

기자

lawyer
*pyŏnhosa*

변호사

merchant
*sangin*

상인

monk
*sudosŭng*

수도승

policeman
*sungyŏng*

순경

postman
*up'yon paedalbu*

우편배달부

secretary
*pisŏ*

비서

student
  *haksaeng*       학생
teacher
  *sŏnsaeng*       선생
waiter
  *kŭpsa*          급사
waitress
  *yŏgŭp*          여급

I am a ........
  *nanŭn ........ imnida*   나는 … 입니다.
  Buddhist
    *pulgyo sinja*    불교신자
  Christian
    *kidokkyo sinja*  기독교신자
  Catholic
    *ch'ŏnjugyodo*    천주교도
  Jew
    *yut'aein*        유태인

Where are you from?
  *kohyangi ŏdi issimnigga?*   고향이 어디십니까?
  Australia
    *osŭt'ŭreillia*   오스트레일리아
  Canada
    *k'aenada*        캐나다
  Denmark
    *denmak'ŭ*        덴마아크
  Germany
    *togil*           독일
  France
    *p'ŭrangsu*       프랑스

| | |
|---|---|
| Italy | |
| *it'allia* | 이탈리아 |
| Japan | |
| *ilbon* | 일본 |
| Netherlands | |
| *nedellandŭ* | 네델란드 |
| Russia | |
| *soryŏn* | 소련 |
| Sweden | |
| *sŭweden* | 스웨덴 |
| Switzerland | |
| *sŭwisŭ* | 스위스 |
| United Kingdom | |
| *yŏngguk* | 영국 |
| USA | |
| *miguk* | 미국 |

## Feelings

| | |
|---|---|
| I am ........ | |
| *nanŭn*........ | 나는 … |
| tired | |
| *p'igonhamnida* | 피곤합니다. |
| happy | |
| *kippŭmnida* | 기쁩니다. |
| sad | |
| *sŭlp'ŭn* | 슬픈 |

hungry
*paeka kop'umnida* 배가 고픕니다.
thirsty
*mogi marŭmnida* 목이 마릅니다.
sleepy
*chollimnida* 졸립니다.
scared (v)
*kŏbi namnida* 겁이 납니다.

## Some Useful Phrases

Where are you going?
*ŏdi kasimnigga?* 어디 가십니까?

Do you speak English?
*yŏngŏrŭl halchul aseyo?* 영어를 할 줄 아세요?

Are you married?
*kihonja isimnigga?* 결혼자 이십니까?

What did you say?
*muŏrago hasyŏssŭmnigga?* 뭐라고 하셨읍니까?

I don't know.
*morŭmnida* 모릅니다.

No.
*aniyo* 아니오.

Wait a minute.
*chamganman kidariseyo* 잠깐만 기다리세요.

Yes.
*ye* 예.

What's the matter?
*wae kŭrŏsimnigga?* 왜 그러십니까?

Where is the restroom?
*hwajangsiri ŏdi issŭmnigga?* 화장실이 어디 있읍니까?

# Accommodation

Although the recent surge in building deluxe, international-standard hotels means that plenty of Hyatts, Sheratons, etc are available (except during tourist seasons of April-May and September-October), travellers looking for convenience, will still come across traditional Korean inns, or *yŏgwan* ( 여관 ). Just a block off of Seoul's main Sogong St, *yŏgwan* featuring heated floors and hard pillows can be found for $10 to $25.

As you travel around Korea look for the *yŏgwan* in the narrow alleyways and streets. The homey atmosphere and often shared courtyard provide a taste of Korean living. Wake up to the cries of early-morning foodhawkers walking the alleys. Don't wear your shoes inside the *yŏgwan* rooms or in the halls.

Where is the ........?
......... *ŏdie issŭmnigga?*    ... 어디에 있읍니까 ?
  hotel
    *hot'el*    호텔
  inn
    *yŏgwan*    여관

I'd like ........
......... *ŭl chuseyo*    ... 을 주세요.
  a room
    *pang*    방
  a single room
    *irinyong pang*    일인용 방

a double room
*iinyong pang*      이인용 방

a room with a bath
*yokshiri tallin pang*      욕실이 달린 방

Where is the ........?
........ *ŏdimnigga?*      ··· 어딤니까?
lift (elevator)
     *elribeit'ŏ*      엘리베이터
bathroom
     *hwajangsil*      화장실
fan
     *puch'ae*      부채
lock
     *chamulsoe*      자물쇠
toilet
     *hwajangsil*      화장실

Please bring ........
........ *chom chuseyo*      ··· 좀 주세요.
cold water
     *naengsu*      냉수
hot water
     *ttŭgŏun mul*      뜨거운 물
mosquito net
     *mogijang*      모기장
blanket
     *tamyo*      담요

May I have ........?
........ *chom chuseyo?*      ··· 좀 주세요.

tea
*cha*                                          차

breakfast
*ach'im siksa*                                 아침 식사

lunch
*chŏmsim*                                      점심

supper
*chŏnyŏksiksa*                                 저녁 식사

the menu
*menyu*                                        메뉴

the bill
*kyesansŏ*                                     계산서

## *Some Useful Phrases*

How much per night?
*harutpamŭi yogŭmŭn
ŏlmaimnigga?*                                  하룻밤의 요금은 얼마입니까 ?

Don't you have anything
cheaper?
*tŏ ssan pangŭn
ŏpsŭmnigga?*                                   더 싼 방은 없습니까 ?

That's too expensive.
*nŏmu pissamnida*                              너무 비쌉니다.

Could I see the room?
*pangŭl poyŏ
chushigessŭmnigga?*                            방을 보여 주시겠읍니까 ?

It's too small.
*nŏmu chaksŭmnida*                             너무 작습니다.

This is fine.
*chossŭmnida*                                  좋습니다.

This is not mine.
*igŏsŭn naŭi kŏshi
animnida*　　　　　　　　이것은 나의 것이 아닙니다.

This is mine.
*kŭ kŏt che kŏs imnida*　　　그것 제것입니다.

Could I have the bill?
*kyesansŏrŭl
chushigessŏyo?*　　　　　계산서 주시겠어요 ?

Would you get me a taxi?
*t'aekshirŭl chaba
chushigessŏyo?*　　　　　택시를 잡아주시겠어요 ?

## Some Useful Words

ashtray
*chaetŏri*　　　　　　　재떨이

chair
*ŭija*　　　　　　　　　의자

clean
*kkaeggŭthan*　　　　　깨끗한

cupboard
*ch'anjang*　　　　　　찬장

curtain
*k'ŏŏt'un*　　　　　　　커어튼

door
*mun*　　　　　　　　　문

dirty
*tŏrŏun*　　　　　　　　더러운

expensive
*pissan*　　　　　　　　비싼

light bulb
*chŏngu*　　　　　　　전구

mirror
  *kŏul*                                          거울
newspaper
  *sinmun*                                        신문
pillow
  *pegae*                                         베개
sleep
  *cha-da* (v), *cham* (n)            자다          잠
stay (v)
  *mŏmurŭda*                                   머무르다
soap
  *pinu*                                          비누
towel
  *sugŏn*                                         수건

## At the Laundry
### Some useful phrases
Where is the nearest
laundry?
  *cheil kakaun set'aksoga
  ŏdimnigga?*                         제일 가까운 세탁소가 어딥니까?
I need it tommorrow.
  *naeil p'iryohamnida*               내일 필요합니다.
Can you mend this?
  *igŏsŭl koch'yŏ
  chushigessŏyo?*                     이것을 고쳐 주시겠어요?
Please iron this.
  *igŏt chom taeriseyo*               이것 좀 다려주세요.

### Some useful words
blouse
  *bŭllausŭ*                                       블라우스

| | |
|---|---|
| button | |
| *tanch'u* | 단추 |
| handkerchief | |
| *sonsugo* | 손수건 |
| ironed | |
| *taryŏ* | 다려 |
| pants | |
| *yangbok paji* | 양복 바지 |
| pressed | |
| *p'ŭresŭhae* | 프레스해 |
| pullover | |
| *p'ulobŏ* | 풀오버 |
| shirt | |
| *waisyassŭ* | 와이샤쓰 |
| skirt | |
| *sŭk'ŏt'ŭ* | 스커트 |
| socks | |
| *yangmal* | 양말 |
| underwear (men's) | |
| *p'aench'ŭ* | 팬츠 |
| zipper | |
| *chip'ŏ* | 지퍼 |

# Getting Around

Stand beside any dirt road in Korea, no matter how bad the road appears, and within a few minutes a public bus or taxi is bound to come along. Getting around Korea is easy if you can read Korean place names or properly pronounce the name of your destination.

Between towns you can go by bus or train. Most intercity buses are air-conditioned and comfortable, although legroom may be a problem for tall westerners. Trains have three classes with *saemaul-ho* being the fastest and most comfortable. *Mugung-hwa* is also comfortable but tends to stop more often, and the milk run class is *wanheng*.

Taxis are metered in Seoul and most other cities and towns. For intercity travel or for long distances, you may have to bargain the fare before getting into the taxi. Watch out for the larger beige 'call taxis' which are about twice as expensive as the smaller green or yellow taxis. To catch a taxi go to the taxi queues in front of major hotels or look for the yellow taxi stands on the streets. Luggage is often put in the back seat with the passenger.

Seoul has a modern and efficient subway system. Buy a map that shows subway stations both in Korean script and romanised so you can point to your destination and get help in the subway. Koreans are invariably helpful in getting foreigners pointed in the right direction.

If travelling by bus north of Seoul or anywhere close to the DMZ separating South and North Korea, do not be alarmed if South Korean soldiers stop the bus and ask to see everyone's ID. Show them your passport or drivers license.

Where is the ........?
........ *ŏdimnigga?*          … 어디입니까?
  train station
    *yok*                     역
  bus stop
    *bŏsŭ chŏngryujang*       버스 정류장
  airport
    *kong hang*               공항
  ticket office
    *maep'yoso*               매표소
  subway station
    *chŏnch'ŏryŏgi*           전철역

When is the ........ bus?
........ *bŏsŭnŭn ŏnje*
*issŭmnigga?*                 … 버스는 언제 있읍니까?
  first
    *ch'ŏt*                   첫
  next
    *taŭm*                    다음
  last
    *majimak*                 마지막

## Directions
Go straight ahead.
  *aphuro ttok paro kase yo*  앞으로 똑바로 가세요.
right
  *parŭn jjokŭro*             바른쪽으로
left
  *oenjjokŭro*                왼쪽으로
north
  *pukjjok*                   북쪽

south
  *namjjok*      남쪽
east
  *tongjjok*      동쪽
west
  *sŏjjok*      서쪽

## Instructions

Let's go.
  *kapsida*      갑시다.
I'm in a hurry.
  *sigan i pappŭmnida*      시간이 바쁩니다.
Please slow down.
  *sokto lŭl chom nŭtch'yŏ
  chuse yo*      속도를 좀 늦춰 주세요.
Please wait here.
  *yŏgisŏ kidaryŏchuseyo*      여기서 기다려 주세요.

Please go to ........
  ........ *kaji kapsida*      … 까지 갑시다.
  the airport
    *konghang*      공항
  this address
    *i chuso*      이 주소
  the bank
    *unhaeng*      은행
  the embassy
    *taesakwan*      대사관
  the town hall
    *shichong*      시청
  the market
    *shijang*      시장

the stadium
    *kyŏnggijang*
경기장

the university
    *taehak*
대학

## Some Useful Phrases

Can we go on foot?
    *kŏrŏsŏ kalsu issŭmnigga?*
걸어서 갈 수 있읍니까?

It's too far to go on foot.
    *kŏrŏsŏ kagienŭn yakkan
    mŏmnida*
걸어서 가기에는 약간 멉니다.

I want to go to the hotel.
    *hot'el kaji t'aewŏda
    chuseyo*
호텔까지 태워다 주세요.

I want to get off at ........
    ........ esŏ naerigo
    ship'ŭndeyo
… 에서 내리고 싶은데요.

I want a ticket to ........
please.
    ........ haeng p'yorŭl
    chuseyo
… 행 표를 주세요.

Does this bus go to ........?
    *igŏsŭn ........ haeng
    ppŏsŭimnigga?*
이것은 … 행 버스입니까?

Where is the rest room?
    *hwajangsiri ŏdi
    issŭmnigga?*
화장실이 어디 있읍니까?

## *Some Useful Words*

| | |
|---|---|
| alley | |
| *kolmok* | 골목 |
| bicycle | |
| *chajŏngŏ* | 자전거 |
| conductor | |
| *chihwija* | 안내양 |
| garage | |
| *ch'ago* | 차고 |
| mechanic | |
| *chikgong* | 직공 |
| petrol | |
| *hwibalyu* | 휘발유 |
| street | |
| *kŏri* | 거리 |
| subway | |
| *chihach'ŏl* | 지하철 |
| timetable | |
| *shiganp'yo* | 시간표 |

# Around Town

Finding addresses in the cities is difficult because many streets are unnamed or unposted. Go to a police box for help or stand on the streetcorner looking at a map, with a puzzled look on your face, and someone, usually a young person, will invariably approach to help you.

City maps are available from the tourist information centre behind City Hall in Seoul. Get your hotel to write out the address of your destination in Korean so you can show it to taxi drivers or passersby.

The main forms of transport within towns are the taxis and public buses. In Seoul, the extensive subway system is very convenient.

Korea is a very safe country. Tourists are very rarely the victims of crime and can walk around town at night without worry. Do, however, be wary of pickpockets on buses.

Where is the ........?
| ........ ŏdie issŭmnigga? | ··· 어디에 있읍니까 ? |
|---|---|
| bank | |
|     ŭnhaeng | 은행 |
| book shop | |
|     ch'aekbang | 책방 |
| embassy | |
|     taesakwan | 대사관 |
| hotel | |
|     hot'el | 호텔 |
| inn | |
|     yŏgwan | 여관 |

| | | |
|---|---|---|
| museum | | |
| *pakmulgwan* | 박물관 | |
| post office | | |
| *uch'eguk* | 우체국 | |
| restaurant | | |
| *ŭmsikjŏm* | 음식점 | |
| temple | | |
| *kwanjaori* | 관자놀이 | |

I want ........
........ sipsŭmnida ... 싶읍니다.

| | |
|---|---|
| to buy | |
| *sago* | 사고 |
| to do | |
| *hago* | 하고 |
| to drink | |
| *masigo* | 마시고 |
| to eat | |
| *mŏkko* | 먹고 |
| to go | |
| *kago* | 가고 |
| to see | |
| *pogo* | 보고 |

## At the Post Office

Although most hotels will handle international mail for guests, you must take parcels to be sent overseas to the International Post Office. Many hotels and some post offices offer a packing service. In Korea mail boxes are painted red.

### Some useful phrases

| | | |
|---|---|---|
| I want ........ | | |
| ........ *chom chuseyo* | … 좀 주세요. | |
| an air letter | | |
| *hanggong up'yŏn* | 항공우편 | |
| a postcard | | |
| *up'yŏn yŏpsŏ* | 우편엽서 | |
| a stamp | | |
| *up'yo* | 우표 | |

| | | |
|---|---|---|
| I want to send it by ........ | | |
| *igŏsŭl ........ ŭro puch'igo ship'ŭndeyo* | 이것을 … 으로 부치고 싶은데요. | |
| airmail | | |
| *hanggongup'yon* | 항공우편 | |
| domestic mail | | |
| *kuknae up'yŏn* | 국내우편 | |
| registered mail | | |
| *tŭnggi* | 등기 | |

Where is the nearest post office?
*kajang kakkaun uch'egugi ŏdi issŭmnigga?*
가장 가까운 우체국이 어디 있읍니까?

I want to send a cable.
*chŏnborŭl ch'iryŏgo hanŭndeyo*
전보를 치려고 하는데요.

I want to buy stamps, please.
*up'yorŭl chuseyo*
우표를 주세요.

How much is the postage to
the United States?
*i p'yŏnchirŭl miguk
ponaenŭnte up'yŏn
yogŭmi olmaimnigga?*
이 편지를 미국 보내는데 우편요금
이 얼마입니까?

What window should I go to
for stamps?
*up'yonŭn ŏnŭ ch'angguesŏ
p'amnigga?*
우표는 어느 창구에서 팝니까?

I want to make a collect call.
*k'ollekt'ŭ k'ollo
put'akhamnida*
콜렉트콜로 부탁합니다.

**Some useful words**

cable
*chŏnpo*
전보

express delivery
*soktal*
속달

letter
*p'yŏnji*
편지

letter box
*uch'et'ong*
우체통

number
*sutja*
숫자

parcel
*sop'o*
소포

telephone
*chŏnhwa*
전화

## At the Bank

The Korean unit of currency, the *won*, is abbreviated **₩**.

Be sure to keep the receipts from currency exchanges so you can re-exchange unused *won* upon departure. The exchange rates are usually more favorable at foreign exchange banks than at hotels. *Won* cannot generally be converted outside of Korea.

### Some useful phrases

I want to change ........

........ *pakugoja hanŭndeyo*
··· 바꾸고 싶은데요.

travellers' cheques
*yŏhaengcha*
여행자

cash
*hyŏngŭm*
현금

Where is the nearest bank?
*cheil kakaun ŭnhaengi ŏdimnigga?*
제일 가까운 은행이 어딥니까?

Where can I cash a travellers' cheque?
*yŏhaengja sup'yorul ŏdisŏ hyŏngŭmŭro pakulsu issŭmnigga?*
여행자수표를 어디서 현금으로 바꿀 수 있읍니까?

What is the exchange rate?
*hwanyulŭn ŏlmamnigga?*
환율은 얼맘니까?

What time does it open?
*messi e mun ŭl yŏmnigga?*
몇시에 문을 엽니까?

I want to cash a cheque.
*sup'yorul hyŏnkŭmŭro pakkwŏjuseyo*
수표를 현금으로 바꿔주세요.

## Some useful words

coins
*tongjŏn*        동전

bank notes
*chip'ye*        지폐

bank draft
*hwanŏŭm*        환어음

branch
*chijŏm*        지점

commission
*susuryo*        수수료

credit card
*k'ŭredit k'adŭ*        크레딧 카드

signature
*sŏmyŏng*        서명

identification card
*sinbunjŭng*        신분증

bank
*ŭnhaeng*        은행

money
*ton*        돈

letter of credit
*shinyongjang*        신용장

## Emergencies

Help me!
*saram sallyŏ yo!*        사람 살려요.

Watch out!
*chuwirŭl chal salp'iseyo!*        주위를 잘 살피세요.

Thief!
*todduknom!*        도둑놈 !

Call the police!
*kyŏngch'arŭl pullŏ
chuseyo!*
    경찰을 불러 주세요.

Call a doctor!
*ŭisarŭl pullŏ chuseyo!*
    의사를 불러 주세요.

# In the Country

## Animals

animal
  *tongmul*　　　　　　　　동물

cat
  *koyangi*　　　　　　　　고양이

chicken
  *tak*　　　　　　　　　　닭

cow
  *amso*　　　　　　　　　암소

crab
  *ke*　　　　　　　　　　게

dog
  *kae*　　　　　　　　　　개

fish
  *mulgogi*　　　　　　　　물고기

frog
  *kaeguri*　　　　　　　　개구리

goat
  *yŏmso*　　　　　　　　염소

horse
  *mal*　　　　　　　　　　말

rabbit
  *chipt'oggi*　　　　　　집토끼

rat
  *chwi*　　　　　　　　　쥐

## In the Country

beach
  *haebyŏn*  해변
cave
  *kul*  굴
grass
  *chandi*  잔디
harbour
  *hanggu*  항구
house
  *chip*  집
island
  *sŏm*  섬
lake
  *hosu*  호수
mountain
  *san*  산
river
  *kang*  강
road
  *kil*  길

rock
*pawi*                              바위
sand
*morae*                            모래
sea
*pada*                             바다
tree
*namu*                             나무
valley
*kolchagi*                         골짜기
waterfall
*p'okp'o*                          폭포

## Weather

fog
*angae*                            안개
rain
*pi*                               비
sun
*t'aeyang*                         태양
snow
*nun*                              눈
wind
*param*                            바람

### Some useful phrases

How is the weather?
*nalssiga ŏttŏssŭmnigga?*          날씨가 어떻습니까?
It's very cold.
*daedanhi ch'upssŭmnida*           대단히 춥습니다.
It's a very hot day!
*onŭrŭn to upchiyo!*               날씨가 상당히 덥군요!

## *Place Names*
### Provinces

| | |
|---|---|
| Cheju-do | 제주도 |
| Chulla-namdo | 전라남도 |
| Chulla-pukdo | 전라북도 |
| Chungchong-namdo | 충청남도 |
| Chungchong-pukdo | 충청북도 |
| Kangwon-do | 강원도 |
| Kyongsang-namdo | 경상남도 |
| Kyongsang-pukdo | 경상북도 |
| Kyungki-do | 경기도 |

### Cities

| | |
|---|---|
| Cheju | 제주 |
| Inchon | 인천 |
| Jinhae | 진해 |
| Jinju | 진주 |
| Kwangju | 광주 |
| Kyongju | 경주 |
| Panmunjom | 판문점 |
| Pohang | 포항 |
| Pusan | 부산 |
| Puyo | 부여 |
| Seoul | 서울 |
| Suwon | 수원 |
| Taegu | 대구 |
| Taejon | 대전 |
| Ulsan | 울산 |

오백원

# Food

The most common Korean foods are *kimchi* and rice. *Kimchi* encompasses several types of pickled vegetables, most commomly Chinese cabbage (*paechu*) or daikon radish (*mu*). *Kimchi* is pickled in garlic and hot pepper and should be eaten with care. Boiled rice is eaten with almost every meal.

*Chuseyo* is used when you want to obtain something and can be translated as 'give me'. To be polite, *chŏm* or 'please' should be added before *chuseyo*.

## Mealtimes
breakfast
  *ach'im*　　　　　　　　아침 식사
lunch
  *chŏmshim*　　　　　　점심
supper
  *chŏnyŏk*　　　　　　　저녁

## Drinks
barley tea
  *boricha*　　　　　　　보리차
beer
  *maekju*　　　　　　　맥주
coffee
  *kŏpi*　　　　　　　　　커피
juice
  *chuusŭ*　　　　　　　쥬스

milk
*uyu*                       우유
wine
*p'odoju*                   포도주

## Fruit

apple
*sagwa*                     사과
chestnuts
*pam*                       밤
lemon
*lemon*                     레몬
orange
*orenji*                    오렌지
peach
*poksunga*                  복숭아
persimmon
*kam*                       감
pear
*pae*                       배

## Seafood

clam
*taehap*                    대합
crab
*ke*                        게
eel
*paemjangŏ*                 뱀장어
fish
*saengsŏn*                  생선

oyster
  *kul*                      굴
shrimp
  *saeu*                     새우

## *Meat*
beef
  *sogogi*                   쇠고기
chicken
  *takkogi*                  닭고기
mutton
  *yanggogi*                 양고기
pork
  *taejigogi*                돼지고기

## *Vegetables*
carrot
  *tangkūn*                  당근
bean sprouts
  *kongnamul*                콩나물
cucumber
  *oi*                       오이
garlic
  *manūl*                    마늘
green onion
  *p'a*                      파
onion
  *yangp'a*                  양파
potato
  *kamcha*                   감자
mushroom
  *pōsōt*                    버섯

radishes
*muu* · 무우
red pepper
*koch'u* · 고추
rice
*ssal* · 쌀
spinach
*sigŭmch'i* · 시금치
tomato
*t'omat'o* · 토마토

## *Condiments*

black pepper
*huch'u* · 후추
mustard
*kyŏja* · 겨자
salt
*sogŭm* · 소금
seasoning
*yangnyŏm* · 양념
soy sauce
*kanchang* · 간장
sugar
*sŏlt'ang* · 설탕
vinegar
*ch'o* · 초

## *Other Food*

bean curd
*tubu* · 두부
bread
*ppang* · 빵

| | |
|---|---|
| dumplings | |
| *mandu* | 만두 |
| egg | |
| *talkyal* | 달걀 |
| ice cream | |
| *aisŭk'ŭrim* | 아이스크림 |
| noodles | |
| *kuksu* | 국수 |
| soup | |
| *kuk* | 국 |

### *Some Useful Phrases*

What do you recommend?
  *mwŏga chossŭmnigga?*  뭐가 좋습니까 ?

How much is the set menu?
  *chŏngshigŭn
  ŏlmaimnigga?*                     정식은 얼마입니까?
The food is cold.
  *i ŭmshigŭn ch'ayo*               이 음식은 차요.
I've had enough, thank you.
  *ta mŏgŏssŭmnida
  komapsumnida*                     다 먹었습니다. 고맙습니다.
Is the water boiled?
  *i mul kurim mul imnigga?*        이 물 끓인 물입니까?
Please bring the bill.
  *kyesansŏ chom kajyŏoseyo*        계산서 좀 가져오세요.
Is service included?
  *sŏbisŭryodo tŭrŏ
  issŭmnigga?*                      서비스료도 들어 있읍니까?
Do you have ........?
  ........ *issŭmnigga?*            … 있읍니까?
Please give me ........
  ........ *chusipsiyo*             … 주십시요.
Please bring ........
  ........ *chom chuseyo*           … 좀 주세요.

## Some Useful Words

baked
  *kuun*                           구운
the bill
  *kyesansŏ*                       계산서
bitter
  *ssŭn*                           쓴
boiled
  *salmŭn*                         삶은

boiled water
  *kurim mul*　　　　　　　　끓인 물

bottle
  *han pyŏng*　　　　　　　　한 병

chopsticks
  *chŏtgarak*　　　　　　　　젓가락

cold
  *ch'an*　　　　　　　　　　찬

cup
  *chan*　　　　　　　　　　잔

delicious
  *masitnŭn*　　　　　　　　맛있는

empty
  *pin*　　　　　　　　　　빈

fork
  *p'ok'ŭ*　　　　　　　　　포오크

fresh
  *singsinghan*　　　　　　　싱싱한

fried
  *p'ŭraihan*　　　　　　　　프라이한

full
  *kadŭkch'an*　　　　　　　가득찬

glass
  *han chan*　　　　　　　　한 잔

hot (temp)
  *toun*　　　　　　　　　　더운

hot (taste)
  *maeun*　　　　　　　　　매운

knife
  *naip'ŭ*　　　　　　　　　나이프

medium
  *pot'ongŭro ik'in*　　　　보통으로 익힌

| | |
|---|---|
| the menu | |
| *menyu* | 메뉴 |
| plate | |
| *chŏpshi* | 접시 |
| rare | |
| *sŏlguun* | 설구운 |
| raw | |
| *nalgŏsui* | 날것의 |
| ripe | |
| *ikŭn* | 익은 |
| rotten | |
| *ssŏkŭn* | 썩은 |
| sour | |
| *sik'ŭmhan* | 시큼한 |
| spoon | |
| *sŭp'un* | 스푼 |
| stale | |
| *sanghan* | 상한 |
| sweet | |
| *talk'omhan* | 달콤한 |
| well-done | |
| *chal ik'in* | 잘 익힌 |

# Shopping

Bargaining is the custom except in department stores, book shops, and posted 'fixed-price' stores. In most cases, start by offering about half the stated price and bargain good naturedly. Remember that you are obliged to buy if the merchant accepts your offer.

If you are just window shopping or otherwise not intent upon buying, don't be the first customer to enter a shop in the morning as it is considered a bad omen for the day's first customer to leave without making a purchase.

In Seoul, look for clothing, sports gear, and luggage bargains in the Itaewon area near the US Army's Yongsan Base. Antique shops are concentrated in the Insadong area near Pagoda Park. Namdaemun Market near the South Gate is the best place to experience traditional Korean bargaining under crowded, arm-slinging conditions.

Where is the ........?
*........ odi issŭmnigga?*　　… 어디 있읍니까 ?

market
  *shijang*　　시장
supermarket
  *sup'ŏmak'et*　　수퍼마켓
book shop
  *sŏjŏm*　　서점
shop
  *jŏm*　　상점
pharmacy
  *yakkuk*　　약국

barber
  *ibalso*                        이발소
tailor
  *yangbokchŏm*                   양복점

I want to buy some ........
  ........ *sago ship'ŭndeyo*     … 사고 싶은데요.
  clothes
    *ot*                          옷
  gems
    *posŏk*                       보석
  gold
    *kŭm*                         금
  pearls
    *chinju*                      진주
  silver
    *ŭn*                          은

## Bargaining

How much is this?
  *igŏsŭn ŏlmaimnigga?*           이것은 얼마입니까?
It's too expensive.
  *nŏmu pissamnida*               너무 비쌉니다.
I'll take this.
  *ikŏt chom chuseyo*             이것 좀 주세요.
How much is it altogether?
  *chŏnbu kapsi
  ŏlmaimnigga?*                   전부 값이 얼마입니까?
Will you deliver it?
  *paedal hae
  chusigessŭmnigga?*             배달해 주시겠읍니까?

I like this one.
*ikŏt chosŭmnida*  이것 좋습니다.
I want something cheaper.
*chom tŏ ssan kŏs ŭro*
*chuseyo*  좀 더 싼것을 주세요.

## Quantities
gram
*gŭraem*  그램
kilogram
*k'ilrogŭraem*  킬로그램
large
*k'ŭn*  큰
less
*poda chŏkun*  보다 적은
litre
*rit'ŏ*  리터
more
*tŏmanŭn*  더 많은
packet
*kurŏmi*  꾸러미
pound
*p'aundŭ*  파운드
small
*chagŭn*  작은
tin
*kangt'ong*  깡통

## Information
dictionary
*sajŏn*  사전

envelope
*pongt'u*     봉투
information
*sosik*     소식
magazine
*chapchi*     잡지
map
*chido*     지도
newspaper
*shinmun*     신문
paper
*chongi*     종이
pen
*p'en*     펜
pencil
*yŏnp'il*     연필
writing paper
*p'yŏnji-ji*     편지지

## Colours

black
*kŏmjŏng*     검정
blue
*ch'ŏng-saek*     청색
brown
*kal-saek*     갈색
green
*nok-saek*     녹색
red
*palgang-saek*     빨강색
white
*hŭin-saek*     흰색

yellow
*norang-saek* 노랑색

## Some Useful Phrases

I'm just looking.
*kugyŏng chom hamnida* 구경 좀 합니다.

Do you have any English books here?
*yŏngŏ ch'aekun issŭmnigga?* 영어책은 있읍니까?

How much is it?
*ŏlmaimnika?* 얼마입니까?

I don't like the colour.
*saekkari maŭme andŭmnida* 색깔이 마음에 안듭니다.

## Some Useful Words

another
*tto hanaŭi* 또 하나의

bad
*nabbŭn* 나쁜

battery
*patteri* 전지

big
*k'ŭn* 큰

black & white film
*hŭk-pa* 흑백 필름

camera
*k'amera* 카메라

cigarettes
*tambae* 담배

cheap
*ssan*  산

clean
*kkaeggŭthan*  깨끗한

colour film
*k'alla p'illŭm*  칼라 필름

dark
*saekkari chit'ŭn*  색깔이 짙은

develop
*hyŏnsang*  현상

dirty
*tŏrŏun*  더러운

good
*ch'akham*  착한

handbag
*songabang*  손가방

hat
*moja*  모자

jade
*ok*  옥

large
*k'ŏdaran*  커다란

long
*kin*  긴

paintings
*kŭrim*  그림

radio
*radio*  라디오

shoes
*kudu*  구두

short
*jjalbŭn*  짧은

| | |
|---|---|
| silk | |
| *myŏngju* | 명주 |
| small | |
| *chakŭn* | 작은 |
| toilet paper | |
| *hwajangji* | 화장지 |
| tooth paste | |
| *ch'iyak* | 치약 |
| twine | |
| *noggŭn* | 노끈 |
| umbrella | |
| *usan* | 우산 |
| useful | |
| *yuyonghan* | 유용한 |

# Health

*Apŭmnida* (or *apayo*) is an all-purpose word that means to hurt or to be sick. Simply state the part of the body which hurts and follow the noun with *apŭmnida*. To say *kasŭm apayo* (chest hurts) means that one's feelings are hurt.

No amount of sanitation can protect the owner's of digestive tracts which have been sheltered from the likes of Korea's spicy hot dishes. Although Korea is generally a sanitary place, extra care should be taken when eating at the many sidewalk foodcarts. If the cook appears unhealthy and the dishes sit in overused soapy water, avoid it.

Western medicines are easily available at *yakbang* (western-style chemists) but may be under unfamiliar brandnames. Traditional Korean medicine shops are called *hanyak bang* and can be recognised by the deer horn and fungi which fill their windows.

Where is the ........?

| ........ *ŏdiimnika?* | … 어디입니까 ? |
|---|---|
| dentist | |
|   *ch'igwaŭisa* | 치과의사 |
| doctor | |
|   *ŭlsa* | 의사 |
| hospital | |
|   *pyŏngwŏn* | 병원 |
| pharmacy | |
|   *yakguk* | 약국 |

I have ........
    *nanŭn ........ i apŭmnida*    나는 … 아픕니다.
  an earache
    *kwiga*    귀가
  a headache
    *mŏriga*    머리가
  a pain here
    *yŏgiga*    여기가
  a sore throat
    *mogiga*    목이

I have ........
    *chŏnŭn ........*    저는 …
  a cold
    *kamgie*
    *kŏllyossŭmnida*    감기에 걸렸읍니다.
  diarrhoea
    *sŏlsaga namnida*    설사가 납니다.
  a fever
    *yŏri namnida*    열이 납니다.

## At the Chemist

Do you have ........?
    *........ issŭmnigga?*    … 있읍니까?
  a bandage
    *pungdae*    붕대
  disinfectant
    *sotongyak*    소독약
  medicine
    *yak*    약

tablets
 *allyak* 알약

tranquilisers
 *chinjŏngje* 진정제

## *Parts of the Body*

arm
 *p'al* 팔

body
 *yukch'e* 육체

breast
 *yubang* 유방

chest
 *kasŭm* 가슴

ear
 *kwi* 귀

eye
 *nun* 눈

finger
 *sonkarak* 손가락

foot
 *pal* 발

leg
 *tari* 다리

neck
 *mok* 목

nose
 *k'o* 코

throat
 *mokkumŏng* 목구멍

tooth
 *ibbal* 이빨

## Some Useful Phrases

I don't feel well.
*momi pulp'yŏn hamnida*　　　몸이 불편합니다.
How do you feel?
*kibuni chom
ŏttŏsimnigga?*　　　　　기분이 좀 어떻습니까?
I have a toothache.
*i ga ap'ŭmnida*　　　　　이가 아픕니다.
Please call a doctor.
*ŭsa chom pullŏ chuseyo*　　의사 좀 불러주세요.
Please call a policeman.
*sun'gyŏong chŏm pullŏ
chuseyo*　　　　　　　순경 좀 불러주세요.
Please take us to a doctor.
*ŭsa ege chom teryŏda
chuseyo*　　　　　　　의사에게 좀 데려다 주세요.
Don't do it!
*chebal haji mase yo!*　　　제발 하지 마세요.

## Some Useful Words

blood
*p'i*　　　　피
break
*pusuda*　　　부수다
breathe
*sumswida*　　숨쉬다
burn (v)
*hwasang*　　화상
cough
*kich'im*　　기침
deaf
*kwimŏkŭn*　　귀먹은

**death**
  *chukŭm* — 죽음

**disease**
  *pyŏng* — 병

**drink (v)**
  *masida* — 마시다

**fever**
  *koyo* — 고열

**head-ache**
  *tot'ong* — 두통

**infection**
  *chŏnyŏm* — 전염

**injection**
  *chusa* — 주사

**itch**
  *karyŏum* — 가려움

**patient**
  *pyŏngja* — 병자

**poison**
  *tokyak* — 독약

**rash**
  *paljin* — 발진

**sprain (v)**
  *ppida* — 삐다

**swell (v)**
  *pup'ulda* — 부풀다

**vomiting**
  *t'ohada* — 토하다

# Time & Dates

Telling time in Korean varies very little from telling time in English. To say it is five o'clock, for example, you take the word for five (see chapter on Numbers), *tasŏt*, add the suffix meaning 'o'clock', *si*, and derive *tasŏsi*. Note that the pure Korean version of numbers is used with hours (*sigan*) and the Chinese-derived version is used with minutes (*pun*) (see chapter on Numbers).

For fractions of the time name the hour first and then the minutes:

5.15
   *tasŏ si ship o pun*         다섯시 십오분

This literally means five (*tasŏt*) + o'clock (*si*) + fifteen (*shipo*) + minute (*pun*).

## Telling Time
What time is it?
   *myŏtsi imnigga?*         몇 시 입니까?
It is ........ o'clock.
   ........ *imnida.*         … 입니다.

## Hours
1
   *hansi*         한시
2
   *tusi*         두시

3
*sesi*      세시

4
*nesi*      네시

5
*tasŏsi*      다섯시

6
*yŏsŏsi*      여섯시

7
*ilkopsi*      일곱시

8
*yŏdŏsi*      여덟시

9
*ahopsi*      아홉시

10
*yŏlsi*      열시

11
*yŏlhansi*      열한시

12
*yŏltusi*      열두시

## Minutes

1 minute
*il pun*      일분

5 minutes
*o pun*      오분

10 minutes
*ship pun*      십분

15 minutes
*ship o pun*      십오분

30 minutes
*sam ship pun*      삼십분

**45 minutes**
*sa ship o pun*                   사십오분

**Now it's 2.15.**
*tusi shipopun imnida*            두시 십오분 입니다.
**It is half past one.**
*hansi pan imnida*                한시 반 입니다.

Korean dates are usually written in the order of year, month, and day. Thus, 20 June 1963 would be written as 63 06 20. Although the Gregorian calendar is now used in Korea, many important holidays follow the traditional lunar calendar. Months in Korean are simply referred to as the '1 month', the '2 month', etc.

## Months
**January**
*ilwŏl*                           일월
**February**
*iwŏl*                            이월
**March**
*samwŏl*                          삼월
**April**
*sawŏl*                           사월
**May**
*owŏl*                            오월
**June**
*yuwŏl*                           유월
**July**
*ch'ilwŏl*                        칠월
**August**
*p'alwŏl*                         팔월

September
  *kuwŏl*  구월

October
  *siwŏl*  시월

November
  *sibilwŏl*  십일월

December
  *sibiwŏl*  십이월

## Days

Today is ........
  *onŭrŭn ........ imnida*  오늘은 … 입니다.

Sunday
  *iryoil*  일요일

Monday
  *wŏryoil*  월요일

Tuesday
  *hwayoil*  화요일

Wednesday
  *suyoil*  수요일

Thursday
  *mogyoil*  목요일

Friday
  *kŭmyoil*  금요일

Saturday
  *t'oyoil*  토요일

holiday
  *hyuil*  휴일

## *Some Useful Phrases*

What day is today?
*onŭrŭn musŭn
yoilimnigga?*     오늘은 무슨 요일입니까 ?

What's today's date?
*onŭrŭn myŏch'il imnigga?*     오늘은 몇일입니까 ?

What time is it?
*myŏtsi imnigga?*     몇 시입니까 ?

When will you come back?
*ŏnche tora oshimnigga?*     언제 돌아오십니까 ?

## *Some Useful Words*

day
  *nal*     날
evening
  *chonyok*     저녁
half past
  *pan*     반
hour
  *sigan*     시간
last week
  *chinan chu*     지난 주
midday (noon)
  *chongo*     정오
midnight
  *chajong*     자정
minute
  *pun*     분
morning
  *ach'im*     아침
next week
  *taŭm chu*     다음 주

**night**
*pam* 밤

**noon**
*chŏngo* 정오

**now**
*ch'igum* 지금

**today**
*onŭl* 오늘

**tomorrow**
*naeil* 내일

**tonight**
*onŭl pam* 오늘밤

**yesterday**
*ŏje* 어제

# Numbers

The first 10 numbers need to be learnt, along with the word
for 100, 1000, 10,000, etc, but after that the pattern is t
combine the first 10 numbers to make larger numbers. T
make the combination 15, take the word for 10 *ship* an
combine it with 5 *o* to derive 15 *shipo*. To say 21, combine 2 *i*
10 *ship*, and 1 *il* to make *ishipil*. Note that there are a few
irregularities.

Although Arabic numerals are used there are two system
of pronouncing cardinal numbers in Korean; pure Korean
and Chinese-derived. Korean numbers (which only go up t
99) are generally used when referring to things and hours
The Chinese-derived numbers are used to count money (th
Korean currency is *won*), days, mileage, or minutes.

| Number | Chinese Numbers | | Korean Numbers | |
|--------|---------|---|--------|------|
| 1 | *il* | 일 | *hana* | 하나 |
| 2 | *i* | 이 | *tul* | 둘 |
| 3 | *sam* | 삼 | *set* | 셋 |
| 4 | *sa* | 사 | *net* | 넷 |
| 5 | *o* | 오 | *tasŏt* | 다섯 |
| 6 | *yuk* | 육 | *yŏsot* | 여섯 |
| 7 | *ch'il* | 칠 | *ilgop* | 일곱 |
| 8 | *p'al* | 팔 | *yŏdŏl* | 여덟 |
| 9 | *ku* | 구 | *ahop* | 아홉 |
| 10 | *ship* | 십 | *yŏl* | 열 |

| Number | Combination | |
|--------|-------------|---|
| 11 | *shipil* | 십일 |
| 12 | *shipi* | 십이 |
| 13 | *shipsam* | 십삼 |
| 14 | *shipsa* | 십사 |
| 15 | *shipo* | 십오 |
| 16 | *shimnyuk* | 십육 |
| 17 | *shipch'il* | 십칠 |
| 18 | *ship'al* | 십팔 |
| 19 | *shipku* | 십구 |

| Number | Combination | |
|--------|-------------|---|
| 10 | *ship* or *yŏl* | 열 |
| 20 | *iship* | 이십 |
| 30 | *samship* | 삼십 |
| 40 | *saship* | 사십 |
| 50 | *oship* | 오십 |
| 60 | *yukship* | 육십 |
| 70 | *ch'ilship* | 칠십 |
| 80 | *p'alship* | 팔십 |
| 90 | *kuship* | 구십 |
| 100 | *paek* | 백 |

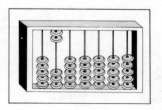

| Number | Combination | |
|--------|-------------|---|
| 200 | *ipaek* | 이백 |
| 300 | *sampaek* | 삼백 |
| 400 | *sapaek* | 사백 |
| 500 | *opaek* | 오백 |
| 600 | *yukpaek* | 육백 |
| 700 | *ch'ilpaek* | 칠백 |
| 800 | *p'alpaek* | 팔백 |
| 900 | *kupaek* | 구백 |
| 1000 | *ch'ŏn* | 천 |
| 10,000 | *man* | 만 |

**Some numbers**

259 – i paek o sip ku 이백오십구
    2 100 5 10 9

2350 – i ch'on sam paek o sip 이천삼백오십
    2 1000 3 100 5 10

## *Some Useful Words*

How many?
  *met*                 몇
pound
  *p'aundŭ*        파운드
ounce
  *onsŭ*            온스
a lot
  *manŭm*         많음
too much
  *nŏmu mani*    너무 많이
enough
  *ch'ungbunhan*  충분한

# Vocabulary

## A

accident – *sago*          사고
aeroplane – *pihaenggi*    비행기
afternoon – *ohu*       오후
age – *nai*           나이
agriculture – *nongŏp*    농업
airmail – *hongkong up'yon*  항공우편
all – *modŭn*         모든
antibiotics – *hangsaeng*  항생제
antique – *koldongp'um*  골동품
apple – *sagwa*       사과
art – *yesul*         예술
ashtray – *chaeddŏri*   재떨이

## B

bad – *nabbŭn*        나쁜
baggage – *suhamul*    수하물
bank – *ŭnhaeng*      은행
barber – *ibalsa*      이발사
basket – *paguni*     바구니
bath – *mokyok*       목욕
bathroom – *hwajangsil*  화장실
beach – *haebyŏn*     해변
beans – *k'ong*       콩
beautiful – *arŭmdaun*  아름다운
bed – *ch'imdae*     침대
beef – *soegogi*     쇠고기
beer – *maekju*      맥주

better – *tŏ choŭn* 더 좋은
bicycle – *chajŏngŏ* 자전거
big – *k'ŭn* 큰
blanket – *tamyo* 담요
bleed – *p'irŭl hŭllrida* 피를 흘리다
book – *ch'aek* 책
bottle – *pyŏng* 병
bowl – *sabal* 사발
boy – *namja* 남자
bread – *ppang* 빵
breakfast – *choban* 조반
bridge – *tari* 다리
broken – *pusŏjin* 부서진
building – *kŏnmul* 건물
burn (v) – *pult'ada* 불타다
bus – *pŏsŭ* 버스
butter – *bŏt'ŏ* 버터
buy (v) – *sada* 사다

## C

cake – *kwaja* 과자
carpet – *yangt'anja* 양탄자
change (money) – *chandon* 잔돈
cheap – *ssan* 싼
chemist (drugstore) –
  *yakbang* 약방
chicken – *tak* 닭
child – *ai* 아이
chopsticks – *chŏtgarak* 젓가락
cigarettes – *tambae* 담배
closed – *tatda* 닫다
coffee – *k'oop'i* 코오피

cold – *ch'an* 찬
colour – *pitggal* 빛깔
come (v) – *oda* 오다
country (nation) – *nara* 나라
crab – *ke* 게
cup – *chan* 잔

## D

dark – *ŏduun* 어두운
dessert – *tijŏŏt'ŭ* 디저어트
diarrhoea – *sŏlsa* 설사
difficult – *ŏryŏun* 어려운
dining car – *sikdangch'a* 식당차
dinner – *chŏngch'an* 정찬
doctor – *ŭisa* 의사
dormitory – *kisuksa* 기숙사
dozen – *han t'asŭ* 한 타스
duck – *ori* 오리

## E

early – *irŭn* 이른
east – *tongjjok* 동쪽
easy – *swiun* 쉬운
eat (v) – *mŏkda* 먹다
egg – *kyeran* 계란
embassy – *taesagwan* 대사관
empty – *pin* 빈
engineer – *kisa* 기사
enough – *ch'ungbunhan* 충분한
envelope – *pongt'u* 봉투
evening – *chŏnyŏk* 저녁
expensive – *pissan* 비싼

## F

| | | |
|---|---|---|
| face – *ŏlgul* | 얼굴 |
| faint – *hŭimihan* | 희미한 |
| far – *mŏn* | 먼 |
| fever – *koyŏl* | 고열 |
| film (photo) – *p'ilrŭm* | 필름 |
| find – *palgyŏnhaenaeda* | 발견해내다 |
| fish – *mulgogi* | 물고기 |
| flight – *pihaeng* | 비행 |
| 'flu – *yuhaengsŏng kamgi* | 유행성감기 |
| fork – *p'ok'ŭ* | 포오크 |
| full – *kadŭkhan* | 가득찬 |

## G

| | |
|---|---|
| girl – *yoja* | 여자 |
| glasses – *angyŏng* | 안경 |
| go – *kada* | 가다 |
| good – *ch'akham* | 착함 |
| goodbye – *annyŏnghi kyesipsio* | 안녕히 계십시오. |

## H

| | |
|---|---|
| head – *mŏri* | 머리 |
| heat – *yŏl* | 열 |
| heavy – *mugŏun* | 무거운 |
| help (v) – *topda* | 돕다 |
| here – *yŏgi* | 여기 |
| hill – *ŏndŏk* | 언덕 |
| hospital – *pyŏngwŏn* | 병원 |
| hot – *toun* | 더운 |
| hotel – *hot'el* | 호텔 |
| hour – *sigan* | 시간 |

**I**

ice cream – *aisŭk'ŭrim*  아이스크림
immediately – *kot*  곧
indigestion – *sohwa pulryang*  소화불량
injection – *chusa*  주사

**J**

jade – *pich'wi*  비취
jewellery – *posŏk*  보석
journalist – *kija*  기자

**K**

key – *yŏlsoe*  열쇠
knife – *naip'ŭ*  나이프

**L**

lake – *hosu*  호수
late – *nŭjŭn*  늦은
lawyer – *pŏpryulga*  법률가
left – *oenp'yŏnŭro*  왼편
letter – *p'yŏnji*  편지
light (weight) – *kabyŏun*  가벼운
like (v) – *choahada*  좋아하다
look – *paraboda*  바라보다
love – *sarang*  사랑
luggage – *suhamul*  수하물
lunch – *chŏmsim*  점심

**M**

map – *chido*  지도
marry – *kyŏlhonhada*  결혼하다

matches – *sŏngnyang*      성냥
milk – *uyu*      우유
minute – *pun*      분
money – *ton*      돈
month – *tal*      달
morning – *ach'im*      아침
music – *ŭmak*      음악
museum – *pakmulgwan*      박물관
mutton – *yanggogi*      양고기

## N

name – *irŭm*      이름
near – *kaggaun*      가까운
needle – *panŭl*      바늘
new – *saeroun*      새로운
noisy – *siggŭrŏun*      시끄러운
noodles – *kuksu*      국수
north – *pukjjok*      북쪽
now – *chigŭm*      지금
number – *sutja*      숫자

## O

old – *nalgŭn*      늙은
open (v) – *yŏlda*      열다
or – *ttonŭn*      또는
orange – *orenji*      오렌지
other – *tarŭn*      다른

## P

pagoda – *t'ap*      탑
pain – *kot'ong*      고통
paintings – *kŭrim*      그림

parcel – *sop'o* 소포
park – *kongwŏn* 공원
passport – *yŏgwŏn* 여권
peach – *poksunga* 복숭아
pepper – *huch'u* 후추
persimmon – *kam* 감
plate – *chŏpsi* 접시
platform – *p'ŭlraetp'oom* 플랫포옴
police – *kyŏngch'al* 경찰
porcelain – *sagikŭrŭt* 사기그릇
pork – *twaejigogi* 돼지고기
post (v) – *usonghada* 우송하다
post office – *uch'eguk* 우체국
postcards – *up'yŏn yŏsŏ* 우편엽서
prescription – *ch'ŏbang* 처방
province – *to* 도

## Q

quick – *parŭn* 빠른

## R

railway – *ch'ŏldo* 철도
rain – *pi* 비
razor – *myŏndok'al* 면도칼
receipt – *yŏngsujŭng* 영수증
rent (v) – *pilrida* 빌리다
repair – *susŏnhada* 수선하다
rest – *swida* 쉬다
restaurant – *ŭmsikjŏm* 음식점
return – *hoegohada* 회고하다
rice (cooked) – *pap* 밥
right (side) – *orŭn* 오른

river – *kang* 강
road – *kil* 길
room – *pang* 방

## S

salt – *sogŭm* 소금
scenery – *kyŏngch'i* 경치
second (time) – *ch'o* 초
shampoo – *mŏrirŭl kamda* 머리를 감다
shoe lace – *kuduggŭn* 구두끈
shop – *kage* 가게
shopping – *changbogi* 장보기
shower – *syauŏ* 샤우어
shut – *tach'in* 닫힌
signature – *sŏmyŏng* 서명
silk – *myŏngju* 명주
sleep (v) – *chada* 자다
slowly – *ch'ŏnch'ŏnhi* 천천히
small – *chakŭn* 작은
smoke (v) – *tambae p'iuda* 담배피우다
snack – *kandanhan siksa* 간단한 식사
snow (v) – *nunioda* 눈이 오다
soap – *pinu* 비누
soup – *kuk* 국
south – *namjjok* 남쪽
soya sauce – *kanjang* 간장
speak (v) – *malhada* 말하다
spoon – *sŭp'uun* 스푼운
stale – *sanghan* 상한
stamps – *up'yo* 우표
stomach – *pae* 배
stop (v) – *mŏmch'uda* 멈추다

street – *kŏri* 거리
student – *haksaeng* 학생
style – *moyang* 모양
sugar – *sŏlt'ang* 설탕
sweet – *talk'omhan* 달콤한
swim (v) – *heŏmch'ida* 헤엄치다

# T

table – *t'akja* 탁자
teacher – *sŏnsaeng* 선생
telegram – *chŏnbo* 전보
telephone – *chŏnhwa* 전화
tell – *malhada* 말하다
temple – *kwanjarori* 관자놀이
thanks – *kamsahapnida* 감사합니다
theatre – *kŭkjang* 극장
there – *kŏgi* 거기
thread – *sil* 실
throat – *mokgumŏng* 목구멍
tickets – *p'yo* 표
toast – *t'ousŭt'ŭ* 토우스트
today – *onŭl* 오늘
toilet – *pyŏnso* 변소
tomorrow – *naeil* 내일
tooth – *i* 이
toothbrush – *ch'itsol* 칫솔
toothpick – *issusigae* 이쑤시개
toy – *changnangam* 장난감
trade – *sangŏp* 상업
train – *kich'a* 기차
travel – *yŏhaeng* 여행
tumbler – *k'ŏp* 컵

## U

ulcer – *kweyang* 궤양
umbrella – *usan* 우산
underground (subway) –
   *chihach'ŏl* 지하철
understand – *aressumnida* 알았읍니다
university –
   *chonghap taehakgyo* 종합대학교
upstairs – *wich'ŭng* 위층

## V

vegetables – *yach'ae* 야채
vinegar – *ch'o* 초
vomit – *t'ohada* 토하다

## W

waiter – *kŭpsa* 급사
waitress – *yŏgŭp* 여급
wage – *imgŭm* 임금
wait (v) – *kidarida* 기다리다
want (v) – *wŏnhada* 원하다
watermelon – *subak* 수박
weather – *nalssi* 날씨
week – *chu* 주
west – *sŏjjok* 서쪽
what – *muŏsŭl* 무엇
when – *ŏnje* 언제
where – *ŏdiso* 어디서
which – *ŏnŭ* 어느
who – *nugu* 누구
why – *wae* 왜
wine – *p'odoju* 포도주

**Y**

year – *nyŏn*　　　　　　　　년
yesterday – *ŏje*　　　　　　　어제
young – *chŏlmŭn*　　　　　　젊은

**Z**

zoo – *tongmulwŏn*　　　　　동물원

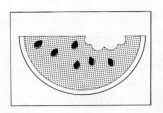

**92 Notes**

## Language survival kits

### China phrasebook
China's official language, Mandarin (*Putonghua*) is covered in this phrasebook. It includes both conventional *pinyin* spellings and Chinese characters for all phrases.

### Tibet phrasebook
Few Tibetans speak English, so it is important to be able to communicate in their language. Tibetan is also spoken in other parts of China, Nepal, Sikkim and Ladakh.

### Nepal phrasebook
Nepali is spoken in parts of India, Sikkim and Bhutan as well as Nepal. This phrasebook includes a special trekking chapter.

### Hindi/Urdu phrasebook
Hindi is spoken in north India; Urdu is spoken in Pakistan. Both languages are closely related so they have been combined in this doubly useful book.

### Sri Lanka phrasebook
This phrasebook covers Sinhala, the official national language of Sri Lanka. It's an ancient language with a complicated script but its pronunciation is not difficult.

### Thailand phrasebook

This phrasebook uses easy-to-follow pronunciation symbols but also includes Thai script. This allows you to 'point and show'.

### Burmese phrasebook

Speaking Burmese will help you make the most of the limited time you are allowed in Burma. This book contains many useful phrases, complete with Burmese script.

### Indonesia phrasebook

A little Indonesian is easy to learn, and it's almost identical to Malay so this book is doubly useful. The rewards for learning some *Bahasa* are far greater than the effort involved!

### Papua New Guinea phrasebook

Pidgin is PNG's lingua franca, also spoken with minor variations in the Solomon Islands and Vanuatu. Pidgin will be especially useful in the countryside and on the islands.

### Swahili phrasebook

Swahili is widely spoken throughout East Africa. This book will be useful whether you are on safari in Kenya or looking for a hotel in Zanzibar.

**Travel Survival Kits**
*Alaska*
*Australia*
*Baja California*
*Bali & Lombok*
*Bangladesh*
*Burma*
*Canada*
*Chile & Easter Island*
*China*
*East Africa*
*Ecuador & the Galapagos Islands*
*Egypt & the Sudan*
*Fiji*
*Hong Kong, Macau & Canton*
*India*
*Indonesia*
*Japan*
*Jordan & Syria*
*Kashmir, Ladakh & Zanskar*
*Kathmandu & Nepal*
*Korea & Taiwan*
*Malaysia, Singapore & Brunei*
*Mexico*
*Micronesia*
*New Zealand*
*Pakistan*
*Papua New Guinea*
*Peru*
*Philippines*
*Raratonga & the Cook Islands*
*Sri Lanka*
*Tahiti & French Polynesia*
*Taiwan*

*Thailand*
*Tibet*
*Turkey*
*Yemen*

**Shoestring Guides**
*Africa on a shoestring*
*North-East Asia on a shoestring*
*South America on a shoestring*
*South-East Asia on a shoestring*
*West Asia on a shoestring*

**Trekking & Walking Guides**
*Bushwalking in Papua New Guinea*
*Tramping in New Zealand*
*Trekking in the Indian Himalaya*
*Trekking in the Nepal Himalaya*

**Phrasebooks**
*Burmese phrasebook*
*China phrasebook*
*Hindi/Urdu phrasebook*
*Indonesia phrasebook*
*Nepal phrasebook*
*Papua New Guinea phrasebook*
*Sri Lanka phrasebook*
*Swahili phrasebook*
*Thailand phrasebook*
*Tibet phrasebook*

**And Also**
*Travel with Children*
*Travellers Tales*

Lonely Planet travel guides are available round the world.
For a copy of our current booklist or a list of our distributors write to:
Lonely Planet, PO Box 88, South Yarra, Vic. 3141. Australia
Lonely Planet, Embarcadero West, 112 Linden St, Oakland,
          CA 94607, USA